THE LIFE AND WORKS OF

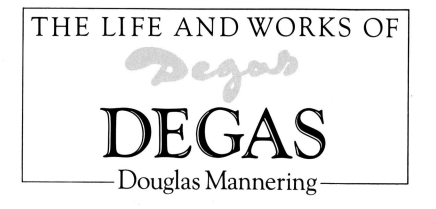

DEGAS

Douglas Mannering

A Compilation of Works from the
BRIDGEMAN ART LIBRARY

SHOOTING STAR PRESS

Shooting Star Press Inc
230 Fifth Avenue, New York, New York 10001

Degas

This edition first published in Great Britain in 1994
by Parragon Book Service Limited

© 1994 Parragon Book Service Limited

ISBN 1 85813 506 0

Printed in Italy

Editorial Director: Lesley McOwan
Designer: Robert Mathias
Production Director: David Manson

EDGAR DEGAS   1835-1917

EDGAR DEGAS WAS BORN IN PARIS on 19 July 1835. He came from a wealthy banking family and had a standard upper-class education at the Lycée Louis le Grand. After briefly studying law, he elected to become an artist, working under approved masters and spending several years in Italy, then regarded as the 'finishing school' of the arts.

By the 1860s Degas was already producing superb portraits, closely observed and characteristically original in composition. But his ambitions were still directed towards conventional success – in 19th-century France this meant having pictures accepted to be shown at the official Salon, which was virtually the only place where an artist could become known to the general public. Consequently Degas painted the kind of works that had most prestige at the Salon: large, detailed set-pieces on historical topics such as *The Young Spartans* (pages 12-13) and *Semiramis Founding a City.*

Only quite late in the 1860s did Degas begin to explore 'modern' subjects, which were regarded by the art establishment as rather trivial and lacking in nobility. However, Degas was somewhat behind his friend and rival Edouard Manet in becoming a 'painter of modern life', and he always restricted himself to a handful of subjects – portraits, the racecourse, the theatre, the orchestra, ladies at the milliner's, laundresses, the nude, and above all the ballet. He tackled each one again and again, often over long periods, constantly experimenting with new approaches; probably the closest analogy is with composers who produce sets of variations on a single theme. Miraculously, Degas is never stale, and his pictures bear a family resemblance without ever looking over-alike.

Degas's techniques were highly original, although they owed something to the great 19th-century vogue for Japanese prints and the up-and-coming art of photography. He portrayed his subjects from unusual angles (often from a very high viewpoint), almost always positioning them off-centre; and instead of neatly tucking peripheral objects within the picture frame, he sliced straight through them. The effect is that of a snapshot, capturing a fleeting moment; the half-seen objects on the edge of the picture give the viewer the illusion that the scene continues beyond the frame. But although Degas's pictures look spontaneous, they were actually carefully premeditated studio productions, built up from many sketches and studies. His was an art that concealed its artfulness.

Degas was an intensely private man, and his life was outwardly uneventful except for his service with the National Guard during the Prussian siege of Paris in 1870-1. He made an extended visit to New Orleans to see his brothers in 1872-3, but although he painted several pictures there, he ignored the exotic and specifically American sides of life in Louisiana, believing that an artist could only produce good work in his proper ambience.

In 1874 Degas made his most celebrated public gesture, becoming one of the principal organizers of an independent exhibition, held in opposition to the Salon. Later it became known as the first Impressionist

Exhibition, because of the prominent place taken by Monet, Renoir and other artists who were painting rapid, atmospheric landscapes in the open air. Degas rather disapproved of their work (he saw the exhibition as 'a Realist Salon'), but he nevertheless contributed to all but one of the eight Impressionist shows between 1874 and 1886. Ironically, he is now often thought of as one of the Impressionists.

Even in the early 1870s Degas was having problems with his sight, and by the 1880s it was deteriorating alarmingly. But he continued to work hard, though increasingly in the less physically demanding medium of pastel. He achieved an undreamed-of variety of colour and textural effects, and his work in pastels is as highly regarded as his oil paintings. This is also true of Degas's sculptures: he translated the dancing girls and nudes he had so often drawn and painted into beautifully modelled little figures.

Degas was always an acerbic personality, cruelly witty, aloof and class-conscious. He never married, though he did have a gift for friendship with a happy few. In the 1890s he became increasingly cranky and isolated, but he was able to work until about 1912. His last years were pathetic: he spent much of his time aimlessly wandering the streets of Paris, famous but indifferent to his fame, and almost oblivious to the World War raging to the north. He died on 27 September 1917.

▷ **The Roman Beggar Woman** 1857

Oil on canvas

THIS WAS PAINTED during Degas's student years in Italy, when he was copying the Old Masters and filling his notebooks with sketches of street life. Accurately observed, and rendered in the approved style of the day, *The Roman Beggar Woman* shows that Degas had already achieved a considerable mastery of technique. Though conventional by his later standards, its off-centre composition would remain one of his characteristic devices.

The picture is also interesting for the temptations that Degas has avoided: the woman is shown in profile, in an attitude of simple dignity, with nothing, except perhaps the crust in the foreground, to suggest her poverty or exploit the picturesqueness of her surroundings. In conventional terms, this meant that Degas had missed some opportunities – which is to say that we are already glimpsing his distinctive, fastidious temperament at work.

◁ **The Bellelli Family** c.1858-61

Oil on canvas

In 1858-9 Degas spent nine months in Florence with his aunt Laura and her husband, Baron Bellelli. He made many drawings and oil and pastel sketches of the family, but only worked them into a single complex composition after he returned to his Paris studio in the rue de Madame. The result was his first indisputable masterpiece, beautifully structured, cool-coloured and full of original touches. In particular, the formal stance of the Baroness and one daughter contrasts with the leg-tucked-under pose of the other and the Baron casually turning round in his seat. Moreover the dog beheaded by the edge of the picture is as daring as any of Degas's later croppings. The gravity of the group is apparently explained by the fact that the Baroness was in mourning for her father (Degas's grandfather), whose picture hangs on the wall behind her. But the Bellelli marriage was also deeply unhappy – Laura complained openly about her husband to her young nephew – and the picture subtly implies the tensions and alienations of the situation.

▷ The Young Spartans c.1860

Oil on canvas

HISTORY PAINTING had enormous prestige in the 19th century, and the young Degas evidently felt that he must try to make his name with big, ambitious pictures. Of the five he finished between 1859 and 1865, *The Young Spartans* is probably the best. The subject and composition are fairly conventional. The Spartans were the most disciplined and militaristic of the ancient Greeks, and both boys and girls were brought up to be hard and strong. Here, the girls are challenging the boys to a wrestling match, while the mothers and Lycurgus, the legendary lawgiver who created the Spartan way of life, look on. But in certain respects Degas is already going his own way, leaving out the usual 'classical' trappings and making his contestants true adolescents, gawky and self-conscious, rather than idealized figures. Pentimenti – ghostly lines, especially among the girls' legs – show how Degas altered the painting over the years. He remained curiously fond of it, proposing some 20 years later to exhibit it beside his modern pictures in the 1880 Impressionist Exhibition.

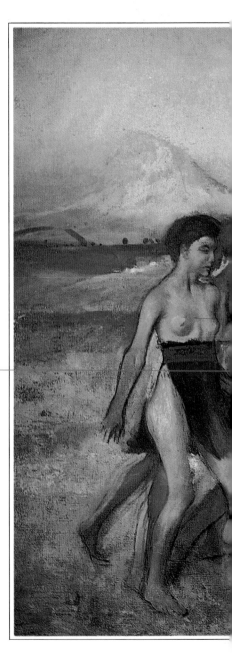

◁ **Portrait of the Artist** c.1863

Oil on canvas

SOMETIMES CALLED *Portrait of the Artist Saluting,* though it is hard to be sure whether Degas has politely taken his hat off to the spectator or to his own mirror image. Self-portraiture is an introspective art; Degas painted fine examples as a young man, but in his thirties he no longer features in his own works. Even these early self-portraits impress as splendid likenesses of a watchful personality who is giving nothing away. Degas's solemn expression, conventional costume and not entirely convincing attitude of being at ease tell us only that he is a thoroughly repectable man about town; perhaps significantly, there is no hint that his profession is one that involves physical activity and becoming spattered with colour. However, it should also be said that Degas's attitude towards himself is in keeping with his dispassionate, unsensational approach to almost all his subjects.

▷ Portrait of Enrique Melida
1863

Oil on canvas

DEGAS OFTEN PAINTED portraits of his artist friends, most of whom came from a similar upper-middle-class background. As portrayed by Degas, they are often the most staid element in a picture of great compositional daring. But in this early portrait, the opposite is true. The unconventional note is sounded by Don Enrique Melida himself, apparently a young bohemian with an unruly thatch of hair, a wry expression and an artist's soft collar. Melida, a Spaniard, nevertheless enjoyed a reasonably successful career as a painter, illustrator and art critic, exhibiting his work in Britain, France and Germany. Degas probably knew him through Leon Bonnat, a painter with whom he had become friendly in the late 1850s, when both were students in Italy; Melida was Bonnat's brother-in-law. In the same year as he painted Melida, Degas executed a splendid portrait of Bonnat which seems to anticipate the great conventional success his friend would later achieve.

◁ **Degas with Evariste de Valernes** c.1864

Oil on canvas

EVEN AS A YOUNG MAN, Degas had a sharp tongue: 25 years after this picture was painted, he wrote to the same Evariste de Valernes apologizing for his asperities and admitting that he had had 'a sort of passion for brutality, which came from my uncertainty and my bad humour'. But he also had a passion for friendship, which he seemed to regard as a sacred bond; Valernes was Degas's friend from their student days together in Italy, and the two men remained in touch until Valernes's death in 1896. Degas painted portraits of many of his friends, but here, exceptionally, he emphasizes the relationship by including himself in the picture. As in other self-portraits (page 14), he seems rather ill at ease; he sits pensively upright, while Valernes, wearing his top hat, lounges nonchalantly, more at home on the canvas than its creator.

Portrait of Princess Metternich c.1865

Oil on canvas

◁ *Previous page 17*

THIS REPRESENTS one of Degas's more curious experiments: painting a portrait from a black and white photograph. The subject was the wife of the Austrian ambassador to France, a woman of some cultivation whose portrait had been painted by the fashionable Winterhalter. Degas, though well-connected, was still a relatively unknown artist, and although he may have seen or spoken to the princess, it is certain that she did not sit for Degas's portrait of her. It was done from a photograph of the princess and her husband which formed part of a visiting card. The card survives, and can be compared with Degas' picture to reveal just how skilfully he modified the reality he painted. Apart from removing the husband, he simplified the princess's dress, softened her features, set her against a floral background, and painted her in warm, quiet colours, transmuting the stiff, formal personage in the photograph into a charming, intelligent woman.

▷ Portrait of James Tissot 1868

Oil on canvas

TISSOT WAS THE KIND of fellow-artist with whom Degas was apt to strike up a friendship – a man of the world with a touch of the dandy, respectful of the conventions but serious about his work. They were close from the 1860s, and Degas's portrait is full of allusions to their mutual interests, notably the German Renaissance painting next to Tissot and the Japanese-style work above it. Tissot himself is shown in an unconventional pose, with his top hat and cloak thrown carelessly on a table behind him, as if he has just come in. In 1871 Tissot emigrated to England, where his glossy, vivid scenes of late Victorian high society made him wealthy and sought-after; in recent years they have enjoyed renewed popularity. Degas invited Tissot to participate in the 1874 Impressionist Exhibition ; Tissot refused, and after that the friendship faded.

◁ At the Races, in Front of the Stand 1868

Oil on canvas

IN THE 1860s Degas gradually discovered his vocation as a painter of modern life, and from the middle of the decade the racecourse became one of the subjects to which he returned again and again. Paris had only just acquired its own racecourse – Longchamps, in the Bois de Boulogne – and racegoing was high fashion; the pretty cluster of blue and white parasols among the spectators suggests the upper-class character of the occasion. Edouard Manet, Degas's friend and great rival as a modern-life artist, also did race paintings, though after Degas and perhaps through his influence – as Degas enjoyed reminding him. Unlike Manet and most other artists, Degas is not interested in the race itself but in the scene just before the start, when the jockeys are trying with varying degrees of success to control their mounts; one has become thoroughly alarmed and has bolted. The picture is among Degas's most inspired compositions, seemingly casual yet worked out to the last detail.

Detail

▷ **The Musicians of the Opéra** 1868-9

Oil on canvas

AT THE TIME it was painted, this would have seemed even more original than it does now. No one had previously thought the orchestra pit worthy of attention, especially in conjunction with a stage performance so brutally marginalized and truncated. In reality the picture is a group portrait of friends, most of them familiar faces at the Degas family's musical evenings. The painting was done for the bassoonist Désiré Dihau, who appropriately occupies its centre. The cellist Pillet sits behind him and the flautist Altes to his left. In front of Dihau, looking out of the picture, is the double bass player Gouffe. The scrolled neck of the instrument, obscuring part of the stage action, became a Degas trademark. High up on the left, the composer Emmanuel Chabrier can be glimpsed in a box. Characteristically, Degas has rearranged the placing of the instruments for the sake of the composition, and has included non-musical friends among the faces in the orchestra.

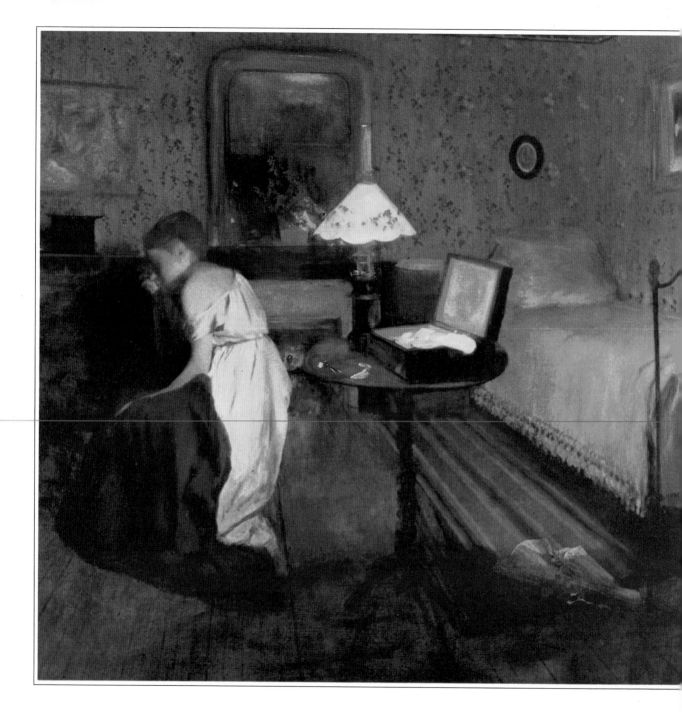

◁ **Interior (Rape)** 1868-9

Oil on canvas

THERE IS NO AUTHORITY for calling this painting *Rape,* but it is easy to see why the title was used. Degas painted nothing else that remotely resembled it in its overt sense of drama, and he steadfastly refused to explain what it was about. The atmosphere is heavy with the threat or memory of violence, although the placing and attitudes of the figures make us conscious that they are alienated from each other. The man's surly, vulpine features, the shadow looming behind him, the woman's lamplit bare shoulder, the objects strewn about, all contribute to the atmosphere, which is all the more oppressive by contrast with the detailed, richly painted interior. It has been suggested that the picture was intended to illustrate Emile Zola's early novel *Thérèse Raquin,* in which Thérèse and her lover Laurent murder Thérèse's husband, only to find their love destroyed by guilt on their wedding night.

▷ **Monsieur and Madame Manet** c.1868-9

Oil on canvas

EDOUARD MANET was two years older than Degas, had begun painting modern subjects before him, and was an artist of comparable stature. The two men were friends after a fashion, but also rivals. Degas was contemptuous of Manet's longing for conventional success, and more than a little jealous of the older man's position as the leader of the painters in revolt against current artistic standards. The tensions in their relationship are suggested by Degas's version of how this painting came to be mutilated: Manet felt that Degas's portrait of his wife at the piano did not do her justice, and simply cut off a strip from the right-hand side – an extraordinary act of vandalism by a fellow-artist. When Degas saw what Manet had done, he walked off with the picture. To add insult to injury, Manet painted his own version of Mme Manet at the piano, to show how it should be done! Manet and Degas eventually made it up, but Degas never got round to repairing the damage to the picture.

△ **Hortense Valpinçon** 1871

Oil on canvas

A MAN OF UNCERTAIN temper, Degas had a way with children and genuinely enjoyed their company. Hortense Valpinçon was the daughter of his school-friend Paul Valpinçon, whose house at Menil-Hubert in Normandy provided a refuge for Degas in times of stress. During the disastrous Franco-Prussian war of 1870-1 Degas enrolled in the Parisian National Guard, serving throughout the Prussian siege of the capital. When Paris was starved out and surrendered, he went to stay with the Valpinçons and painted this portrait of Hortense in a straw hat, pinafore and shawl; her plain dress is in strong contrast to the floral tablecloth, wallpaper and other materials. Here Degas has performed a near-impossible feat, creating a portrait of a child that is colourful and utterly charming without being in the least sentimental.

△ **Jeantaud, Linet and Laine** 1871

Oil on canvas

THIS IS ONE OF DEGAS'S most inspired compositions, ingenious in the extreme and yet showing no signs of strain. On the contrary, these three smiling, relaxed young men seem to have been caught in momentary, natural poses, as if in a photograph. They are debonair men about town who have put behind them the grim circumstances in which they met – as members of Henri Rouart's battery during the siege of Paris, along with Degas himself. Degas became particularly friendly with the engineer Jeantaud (the central figure in the picture), often visiting the family and meeting and painting both Madame Jeantaud (page 00) and Jeantaud's cousin, the Viscount Lepic. Degas's *Place de la Concorde,* showing Lepic with his daughters, was a particularly celebrated picture that has disappeared (probably destroyed during the Second World War) and now exists only in reproduction.

▷ **The Dance Foyer at the Opéra** 1872

Oil on canvas

DEGAS' LIFELONG DEVOTION to the ballet as an artistic subject began at about this time, and *The Dance Foyer* was certainly his earliest large-scale work in the genre. Here he shows a single moment at a rehearsal in the Paris Opéra's practice rooms in the rue Le Peletier. The dancer is taking up her position, the master prepares to call out his instructions, and a fiddler sits ready to provide the necessary accompaniment. Some dancers watch; others go about their business; through the open door, a glimpse of tulle and a leg stretched out parallel to the principal dancer's reveals that the instant 'snapshot' look of the painting is an illusion. The noble proportions of the room, the sharp drawing and the soft, harmonious, light-filled atmosphere give the picture a calm, classic quality.

◁ **The Cotton Market** 1873

Oil on canvas

IN HIS MATURITY, Degas travelled very little. His longest and furthest expedition was to New Orleans, a city in the American South, with strong French connections, where his brothers René and Achille were in the cotton trade. Here Degas has painted a picture of business activity that is not specifically American except for the raw material which the men are sampling and discussing. It is also a group portrait. The seated figure testing a hank of cotton is Michel Musson, René Degas's father-in-law; René is reading the *Times Picayune* newspaper; Achille lounges against an open window. The composition is highly complex, capturing a scene of intense and varied activity while solving the problems posed by including many black outfits in a single scene without overlapping; the mass of brilliant white cotton is an important element in the low-key colour scheme. Degas hoped to find a buyer from Manchester (England's 'cotton capital') for the picture; instead it became the first of his works to be purchased by a French public museum, in 1878.

▷ **The Rehearsal** 1873-4

Oil on canvas

HAVING PERFECTED one
approach to ballet in *The Dance
Foyer of the Opéra* (pages 30-31),
Degas moved on artistically
almost at once. This is another
airy, light-filled scene, but in
most other respects it is very
different and more daring in
its effects. Attention is no
longer concentrated on the
ballet master and his charges;
they perform as gracefully as
ever, but in the background.
In the foreground, but off-
centre, a dancer sits in
workaday pose while an
elderly dresser makes some
adjustment to a fellow dancer's
costume; all three have their
backs to the performers, and
the standing dancer is sliced in
two by the edge of the
painting. These cut-offs, so
important for the effect of
accident and spontaneity that
Degas sought, are especially
pronounced here: the staircase
virtually blots out one of the
dancers, while another is seen
only as a pair of legs coming
down to join the rehearsal.

▷ The Rehearsal on Stage 1873-4

Paper mounted on canvas

DEGAS WAS ALWAYS less concerned with 'the glamour of the theatre' and this rehearsal on stage is even less reverently treated than the other *Rehearsal* (pages 34-35). In the middle ground, the dance master is passionately involved in his work, and the dancers are doing their best to perform beautifully; but the scenes in front of the wings are down to earth. A girl stretches and yawns without any signs of balletic elegance; another adjusts the strap of her shoe; a third tries to relax her feet by hanging on to a stage flat. The postures of the men watching also suggest that the aesthetic quality of the spectacle has long since ceased to interest them. No less than two double-bass scroll-tops rear up cheekily at the front of the scene. Degas made three versions of this picture, which is built up in pastel and oils over an ink drawing.

△ **Two Dancers on Stage** 1874

Oil on canvas

THOUGH HE USED a great many devices to give his works a spontaneous appearance, Degas was essentially a studio artist who carefully worked out his compositions; wandering about backstage, making sketches and notes, and taking photographs. His complex designs were created by integrating individual figures and groups, so masterfully that it is hard to believe that 'the moment' he records never existed. Here the two dancers are unmistakably the same girls as the ones being strenuously rehearsed on pages 36-37. A memory of the characters in that work may qualify our perception of this painting, which otherwise stands as one of his few ballet pictures in which there is no kind of ironic comment on the contrast between stage illusion and reality.

▷ **The Dance Class** c.1874

Oil on canvas

FROM DEGAS'S HUGE output of ballet pictures it would be hard to be sure that any such thing as a male dancer existed. Jules Perrot is one who does appear, but only in old age, as the dancing master in this painting. Leaning on the stick with which the master would call for attention or beat time, Perrot is a commanding figure. The eye is drawn first to him and then to his obedient pupil; but after that the steep perspective takes us further into the room, where a blue-sashed dancer adjusts her costume, and then down to the cluster of restless girls and waiting mothers at the end; one dancer, who has perhaps earned a rebuke, is being consoled by her mother. Gradually we realize that the strength exuded by Perrot (and reinforced compositionally by the upstanding marble pilasters) is undermined by the most of the details, culminating in the girl in the foreground leaning forward to scratch her back, the watering can in the corner and the little dog lurking suspiciously round the dancer with the fan.

◁ Dancer Posing for a Photograph 1874-5

Oil on canvas

IN 1874 DEGAS emerged in an unexpected role, as one of the most active organizers of the first Impressionist Exhibition. During the early 1870s he was also prolific and highly creative, especially in his treatment of ballet subjects. Among other things, he took pains to explore the effects created by the light coming from directly behind the figures and objects in a scene. Here, the icy quality of the light, penetrating the windows and translucent curtains, combines with the austere vertical-horizontal division of the picture to create a sense of the chilliness and bareness of the studio. The dancer is holding a position in front of a large looking-glass which is just visible on the right-hand edge of the picture. We might suppose that she is completely self-absorbed, but Degas's only certain reference to the work – in 1879 – describes it as 'at a photographer's studio – dancer'.

△ **Madame Jeantaud at a Mirror** c.1875

Oil on canvas

THIS CURIOUS and intriguing double portrait has a sketchy quality that might lead one to suppose that it is unfinished, or at any rate too cursorily painted to satisfy conventional tastes. But since Degas presented it to Mme Jeantaud, we must assume that she was pleased with it, though he did also paint a more formal portrait of her a couple of years later. Mme Jeantaud was the wife of Degas' wartime comrade, the central figure in *Jeantaud, Linnet and Laine* (page 20), and the artist became an intimate friend of the family. Mme Jeantaud is shown in outdoor clothes, seemingly checking her appearance before venturing forth. But this is merely the excuse Degas needs to show her in elegant near-profile and, rather more sombrely, full-face. Though Degas's art is generally anti-Romantic, perhaps there is a hint here of the Romantic fascination with the 'double' or alter ego.

◁ **Absinthe** 1876

Oil on canvas

ONE OF DEGAS'S best-known paintings, perhaps because it looks more like an anecdotal or 'message' picture than most of his works. The glass in front of the woman certainly holds absinthe, a green 'mother's ruin' whose ravages were so severe that it was eventually prohibited by the government. The woman's air of disillusion and a certain dreariness in the atmosphere make it easy to believe that Degas was making a moral point; but possibly, as with *Interior* (pages 24-25), he was inspired by Emile Zola's just-published novel *L'Assommoir,* which dwelt on the place of drink as a temptation and a consolation in the lives of the poor. Degas's cool colours emphasize that this is not a merry café scene, but the thrusting diagonal slabs of tabletops play a critical role in creating a sense of strength and vigour to balance the figures. The woman was modelled by the actress Ellen Andrée and the man by Marcellin Desboutin, a bohemian artist friend of Degas and the Impressionists.

On the Beach 1876

Paper mounted on canvas

▷ *Overleaf pages 24-25*

COMING ACROSS a painting like this causes a small shock – and the realization that Degas's mature art is almost exclusively one of the Great Indoors. Though he was a moving force behind the first, revolutionary Impressionist Exhibition of 1874, he was never an Impressionist in the same sense as Manet and Renoir, who painted rapidly and freely in the open air to capture the atmosphere of a landscape. Like many of Degas's works, *On the Beach* has a deceptively casual air (for example through the apparently random scattering of clothing), but in fact it was carefully composed, and painted in the studio. The figures are boldly outlined rather than blending into the landscape, Impressionist-style. The girl slumped on the sand and the nurse patiently combing her hair are beautifully observed; the subject was one that Degas would often return to in later life. The two main figures capture the attention so completely that it is easy to overlook the activities going on elsewhere – so varied that they might be a parody of seaside pleasures.

△ **Ballet Scene from 'Robert the Devil'** 1876

Oil on canvas

ALTHOUGH THIS PAINTING is reminiscent of *The Musicians of the Opéra* (page 23), the greater space allotted to the stage makes it significantly different. Our attention is divided between the musicians and the ballet scene, so that we become aware of the incongruous relationship between 19th-century evening dress and the 'medieval' extravagance of the opera. The scene is from Meyerbeer's *Robert the Devil,* which was then a 40-year-old work from the Romantic era, which Degas and his contemporaries were in full reaction against. And so he has chosen to portray the most absurd moment in the piece, when the ghosts of unchaste nuns tempt Robert to use diabolic means to gain access to his lady love. Down in the pit, the musicians get on with their jobs, while at the extreme left Degas' banker friend Albert Hecht ignores the proceedings on stage and focuses his opera glasses on somebody in the circle or a box.

▷ **Café-Concert at Les Ambassadeurs** c.1876-7

Pastel over monotype on paper

THIS LITTLE PICTURE is one of Degas's most effective 'snapshots', apparently capturing a unique moment, as always, this is an illusion. The Théâtre des Ambassadeurs was the site of large open-air entertainments in the Champs Elysées. Here we are looking over the front rows and orchestra pit, with its dark but firmly outlined figures, towards the figures on stage. Line and colour could hardly come closer to suggesting music, badinage, noise and bustle. As in *The Musicians of the Opéra* (page 23), the scrolled head of the double bass rears up above the line of the stage. The picture started as a print, taken from a drawing made on a metal plate (called a monotype because only one perfect copy was possible), which Degas then worked on with pastels; he often used this technique, especially for ballet scenes.

◁ **Dancer with a Bouquet Curtseying** c.1877

Pastel on paper

DEGAS MADE SEVERAL pastels of this subject, evidently fascinated by the stark effects created by the footlights on the figure of a dancer who has moved close up to them to acknowledge the audience's applause. Here, the performance is over. Holding the bouquet she has just been given, the prima ballerina curtseys. This is her moment of triumph, and the groups of dancers and 'orientals' with parasols are posed statuesquely but at a discreet distance behind her. By contrast with her flower-spangled person, the dancer's face tells us less about the sweetness of success than about the strain imposed by a long performance. Another discordant note, typical of Degas, appears on the left, where the dancers seem to be indifferent to stage appearances: one scratches herself, while the other steps out, perhaps impatient to receive her own share of the applause.

▷ Women in Front of a Café 1877

Pastel over monotype

WHEN THIS INCISIVE PICTURE of life 'on the town' was shown at the third Impressionist Exhibition in 1878, many spectators were shocked: the women on the café terrace, dressed in cheap finery, were undoubtedly prostitutes, chattering away, but keeping an eye open for customers among the passers-by. The exhibition audience would have been even more shocked if they had known that at this time Degas was making a series of monotype prints of life in a brothel; and the prints would have been all the more offensive to 19th-century opinion for being unpornographic, unglamorous and wryly humorous. Degas was also interested in other Parisian entertainments such as the *Café-Concert at Les Ambassadeurs* (page 49). The picture shown here was done by printing an ink drawing on the paper and then working over it with pastels (see page 36).

▷ **Lala at the Cirque Fernando** 1879

Pastel on paper

MISS LALA WAS ONE of the most sensational performers of her day, first seen in Paris at the beginning of 1879. She opened at the Cirque Fernando in the Boulevard Rochechouart, and Degas went to see her act several times. Her specialities included hanging upside down from a trapeze and, as here, being hauled up to the roof by a rope, which she hung on to by her teeth. A canon was suspended at the other end of the rope, and at the climax of the performance it was fired. Degas made a number of preparatory studies, of Lala and of the roof structure, before completing this painting and an equally lovely version in pastel. As well as showing the performance from a low viewpoint, Degas has cunningly placed the woman high up in one corner of the picture, reinforcing our sense that she is daringly far above us.

◁ **At the Stock Exchange** c.1878

Oil on canvas

IN THE LATE 1870s, Degas's interest in capturing nuances of class and characterizing his subjects through their 'body language' was at its most intense. This study of men of wealth and influence operating on the Parisian Bourse (Stock Exchange) is a rarity among his works. The only comparable picture, *The Cotton Market, New Orleans* (pages 32-33), is as much a family group portrait as a scene of business activity. *At the Stock Exchange* has far fewer participants, but they are all closely involved with one another. The principal figure is Ernest May, a Jewish banker who was also a discriminating art collector and admirer of Degas's work. With its air of conspiratorial intimacy, the picture is not entirely friendly; this may be an indication of Degas's latent anti-semitism (which only surfaced during the Dreyfus affair in the 1890s) or, more likely, a rather disdainful response to the world of financial wheeling and dealing.

◁ Portrait of Henri Michel-Lévy 1879

Oil on canvas

IN THIS PICTURE Degas brings vividly to life a now-forgotten fellow-painter whom he had known for some years. Michel-Lévy is said to have been the model for the man in Degas's strangely menacing *Interior* (pages 24-25), and takes up a similar pose here, looking older but also more agreeable than in the earlier picture. By contrast with Degas's portrait of James Tissot (page 19), who could pass as a visitor in his own studio, Michel-Lévy is obviously at home and is surrounded by the tools of his trade. An odd inclusion is the dummy, which seems to have been the model for the female figure in the painting next to Michel-Lévy; some have seen this as an ironic comment on the authenticity of painting 'from life'. Michel-Lévy painted a portrait of Degas and exchanged it for this picture; later, like several of the artist's friends, he was tempted by the steep rise in the prices paid for Degas's works and incurred his wrath by selling it.

▷ Jockeys Before the Start c.1879

Essence on cardboard

THIS VERY LARGE PICTURE was not done in conventional fashion, in oils on a canvas, but on cardboard with 'essence' – pigments mixed with oils of a much thinner texture than the traditional linseed. Hence the distinctive look of *Jockeys Before the Start*. It is also one of Degas's most audacious compositions, taking his characteristic devices to the limit. The pole in the foreground slices right through the horse's head, while most of its hindquarters are cropped. The left-hand side of the scene is left almost entirely empty, and the almost straight horizon completes the division of the picture into near-rectangular areas. Such is Degas's mastery that he has broken most of the rules known to any diligent art student, and has produced a masterpiece.

◁ **Lady Putting on Her Gloves** c.1879

Oil on canvas

IT SEEMS APPROPRIATE to call this *Lady* – rather than *Woman – Putting on Her Gloves,* for there is a very strong feeling throughout Degas's work for the difference between the two types of female. The lady is interesting for her dress and personality, with her own distinctive attitudes and gestures; the woman is working-class, of visual interest when plying her trade (like the girls ironing, page 63) or as a naked, anonymous creature. The illusion that these were two separate species seems to have been shared by Degas. In the 1870s he was particularly concerned to capture nuances of social behaviour. Here the lady seems about to rise at the end of a social visit, of which we have been granted an illicit glimpse through a doorway. The model for the painting may have been the American artist Mary Cassatt, with whom Degas had a long and close friendship.

△ **Portrait of
Edmond Duranty** 1879

Watercolour, gouache
and pastel on canvas

THIS IS A LARGE and ambitious
portrait, of a kind usually
associated with oil painting.
But Degas has used a
fascinating mixture of
techniques which give the
picture its varied texture. After
underpainting in watercolour,
he has used gouache (opaque
watercolour, or 'distemper'),
especially for the shelves
behind Duranty. The blue
book and the other objects on
the desk are painted with a
pastel-water mixture. The
sitter himself is mainly
modelled in pastel. The result
is more than a technical *tour de
force:* Duranty was a close
friend of Degas, who
portrayed him with
considerable sympathy and
insight in his working
environment. As a novelist and
art critic of the *Gazette des
Beaux Arts,* Duranty
championed the 'realist'
tendencies in the art of his
time, and his pamphlet *The
New Painting* (1876) is thought
to have greatly influenced
Degas. As in so many of
Degas's studies of creative
people, Duranty seems to be
not just surrounded but
apparently trapped by his
work, perhaps reflecting
Degas's own sense of the
lonely isolation of the artist.

◁ **Portrait of Diego Martelli** 1879

Oil on canvas

DEGAS'S PORTRAITS of Martelli and Duranty (page 59) might almost have been intended as a contrasting pair. Whereas Duranty is almost overwhelmed by manuscripts, prints and books, Martelli's work is separate from him and unthreatening, despite its bohemian disorder. The pipe on the table and the slippers on the floor also suggest that Martelli's life is not dominated by his work. Nevertheless he was an influential Italian critic who championed realism and, in the course of extended stays in Paris during 1878-9, became a friend and admirer of Degas. The artist has adopted a high viewpoint that emphasizes Martelli's portliness and displays the contents of the table-top. Degas had now reached the peak of his achievement as a portraitist, showing the pictures of Martelli, Duranty and Michel-Lévy (page 56) at the fourth Impressionist Exhibition of 1879.

▷ **The Close of an Arabesque** c.1880

Pastel and oil on paper

FOR ONCE, DEGAS has recorded a ballet performance without introducing some note of irony or incongruity into it. The dancers have been allowed their moment of triumph, and the illusion that all is grace, glamour and beauty remains unbroken. Comparisons with pages 36-37 and 39 will reveal just how unlike Degas such a treatment was. But we need not suppose that his habitual insistence on boredom, exhaustion and other realities of a dancer's life reflected a lack of sympathy: rather it was the fellow-feeling of the artist, who must also undergo a painfully long apprenticeship in order to become an adept, moving backwards and forwards between the banalities of everyday life and rare moments of glory. This, at least, is one of the glories. Clutching a bouquet, the dancer has just swept into a final arabesque, poised on one leg, with the other thrust out level behind her and her arms outstretched. She has put a mysteriously long distance between herself and the rest of the cast, and is presumably about to be overwhelmed with applause.

◁ **Breakfast After a Bath** 1883

Pastel on paper

DEGAS'S INTEREST in the female nude became increasingly obsessive during the early 1880s, focusing on the rituals of bathing, drying and combing the hair. In most examples the woman is shown on her own, the absence of social contact serving to emphasize the pure animality of the figure. But here a servant brings the newly-emerged woman a cup of coffee, apparently indifferent to her state of nakedness. The contrast between vigorous physical health and the impression of slow-moving feebleness made by the servant is a central, 'anecdotal' feature of the picture. In it the pastel has been built up in layer after layer, giving an effect of incomparable richness; the sensuousness of the bather's flesh, the towel and the rich fabrics contrast strongly with the relatively drab attire of the woman waiting with the cup.

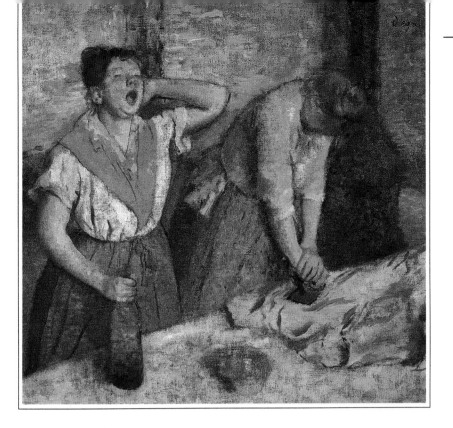

△ **Women Ironing** c.1884

Oil on canvas

DEGAS BEGAN TO PORTRAY laundry scenes such as women ironing in 1869, and this became one of the themes to which he returned from time to time, reworking old efforts and inventing new effects. In popular fancy, laundresses were frilly, flighty young things, easily available to a gentlemen with a roving eye. The availability was real enough, since the women were miserably poor and worked for a pittance, but Degas insists that these are above all big, strong working women. One bears down on the iron with both hands, in an attitude that shows she is using all her strength; the other is yawning and stretching, her hand grasping a bottle – either a bottle of wine or a bottle used to sprinkle water on the ironing. As usual, Degas insists on realities but remains detached, concerned only to create a work of art from his own times that would be as classically structured as any Old Master painting.

◁ **Reading the Letter** c.1884

Pastel on paper

THIS PASTEL IS ABOUT as close to explicit comment on social conditions as Degas ever came. At first sight 'reading the letter' makes the scene part of some untold drama in the laundresses' love-lives; however, the title has become attached to the picture for no particularly good reason, and the piece of paper may well be a laundry list. Uncharacteristically, Degas has shown the working environment in detail, so that each stage of laundering is represented: the heap of dirty washing, the clothes hanging up to dry, the stove used for heating the irons, and the pressed and folded shirts on the table. Moreover, the woman reading is not sitting hand on hip, but holding an aching side, and her companion is leaning against the table in a position people use to rest their backs. Yet, though all of this can be inferred – along with the steamy, unhealthy atmosphere – Degas excludes any note of indignation from the scene.

Jockeys in the Rain c.1886

Pastel on paper

▷ *Overleaf pages 66-67*

ONCE EVERY FEW YEARS, Degas' interest in horses and jockeys flared up again; but although the finished works he produced were new, they were often based on studies made much earlier. Some of the poses in this pastel go right back to drawings made in the 1860s, when Degas first explored the subject. The composition is typically audacious, dividing the picture into two diagonals: the five mounts and their riders are crowded into one, leaving the other bare except for an expanse of soggy greenery. The impression of slanting rain, misting the view and unsettling the horses, is brilliantly created, but there are other streakings and hatchings in the picture which give it a remarkable textural variety. These are perhaps the most aristocratic thoroughbreds Degas ever portrayed, with keen, small heads and delicate fetlocks; by contrast, the jockeys are, for all their bright silks, anonymous and uninteresting.

◁ **The Tub** 1886

Pastel on cardboard

THIS IS ONE OF DEGAS'S most celebrated images of a woman at her toilet. It belonged to a set of ten pastels which the artist showed at the eighth Impressionist Exhibition in 1886, causing a good deal of controversy. Instead of goddesses or coy nymphs, Degas showed anonymous but obviously contemporary women going about their ablutions in a matter-of-fact fashion, unconscious of any observer. Degas himself described it as being 'as if you looked through a keyhole', by which he also implied that there was no element of deliberate erotic display in what was seen. This pastel is one of his last experiments with a high viewpoint and disconcertingly prominent but 'cut off' objects such as the shelf or table-top on the right, which mark a climax of Japanese influence on his work. Moreover, no Japanese bathhouse scene has such a solid, beautifully light-modelled figure at its heart.

△ **Woman in the Tub** c.1886

Pastel on paper

THIS MAY BE one of the series of pastels, including *The Tub* (page 69), shown by Degas at the eighth and final Impressionist Exhibition in 1886; even if it is not part of that series, it is similar in approach and date. It is a much warmer work than *The Tub* and would not look out of place beside nudes by Boucher and Renoir. However, Degas scrupulously avoids the element of self-display that is always present in their female figures: the girl is genuinely preoccupied with drying herself, not with being seen. The shallow tin basin, which the French called *le tub,* was indispensable in a cramped apartment with no bathroom. The bather could crouch, kneel or stand in it – all poses which Degas was at pains to capture.

▷ **Portrait of Hélène Rouart** c.1886

Oil on canvas

HÉLENE WAS THE DAUGHTER of Henri Rouart, a wealthy industrialist who had been at school with Degas. However, the two men became fast friends only when they served in the same artillery battery in the 1870-1 war. Degas painted Henri with his little daughter Hélène in the 1870s; he became enthusiastic about painting her as an adult when the Rouarts visited Venice and he imagined Hélène as one of the red-haired beauties portrayed by the great Renaissance Venetian artists. In the event, although she is the ostensible subject of the painting, her father is equally present. She is in his study, resting on his grand chair and surrounded by the *objets d'art* of which he was a passionate collector. Degas has deliberately exaggerated their size. Unlike Duranty (page 59) and other sitters, Hélène is surrounded by objects that are part of her father's, not her own, life.

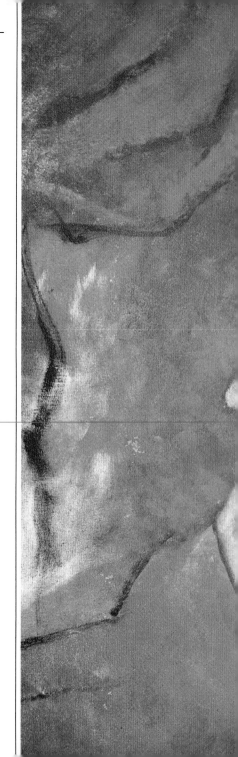

▷ **Combing the Hair** c.1890

Oil on canvas

DEGAS WAS FASCINATED by almost every aspect of women at their toilet, with or without servants to help them. He studied the actions involved in combing someone else's long hair – and putting up with being combed – in his painting of 1876, *On the Beach* (pages 44-45), where the people involved are a young girl and her nanny. Among other memorable images of the subject are the pastel of a nude having her hair combed (c.1886, in the Metropolitan Museum of Art, New York) and this splendid study. It is evidently unfinished, although Degas's habitually contrived 'casualness' may make us question the validity of such a statement. Unlike the earlier pictures, this one is ultra-energetic, with the girl holding her hair to stop it from being pulled out by the roots, while her attendant vigorously combs right through its length. Once again Degas proves himself a master at capturing physical action; but his painting is also a kind of symphony in reds, like a stronger version of the 'nocturnes' of his friend Whistler.

◁ **Woman Drying Herself** c.1890-5

Pastel on paper

WITH ITS LONG, slashing strokes and rich colouring, this wonderful picture seems to have been executed in a blaze of frenzied activity. Given Degas's outlook, the frenzy is almost certainly an illusion; but his command of pastel effects and textures is breathtaking. By this time his eyesight was very poor, and this may account for the bolder, broader style he adopted, although not for the stronger, less naturalistic use of colour. The model's pose is an almost violent version of the many studies made by Degas of women drying their backs, an activity which created postures and revealed muscular tensions far removed from conventional ideas of the nude. Degas also modelled many of his nudes in clay and had them cast as bronzes; they are remarkable works – as remarkable as his better-known ballet figures – with a special place in the history of modern sculpture.

△ **After the Bath** c.1895-1900

Pastel and gouache on cardboard

PAINTED DURING the final period of Degas' artistic career, when he was more than half blind and mainly working from a combination of memory and instinct. This sad situation, rather than any meditated change in Degas' stylistic preferences, may account for the blurred, glorious richness of the colour and the densely worked surface; opinions on this subject differ sharply. Here we have a glimpse of Degas's working methods, for the grid of vertical and horizontal lines, which he used as an aid to transfer the basic image from a preparatory study, is still visible. The subject – a naked woman drying her back – is one of Degas's favourites, creating poses that were necessarily free from artifice and challenging the artist to create entirely new compositions as valid and satisfying as those of the classics.

◁ **Dancers in Blue** c.1899

Pastel on paper.

DEGAS CONTINUED to experiment during the 1890s, even producing some coloured prints and oil paintings of landscapes. But the bulk of his output comprised dancers and studies of the nude, subjects which his long experience enabled him to tackle successfully in spite of his semi-blindness. In this late period Degas's style changed radically. In pictures like the one shown here, the figures are large and viewed close up, filling the picture area in a fashion very different from that of his earlier works. This close-upness makes it hard to decipher the scene: though the matter-of-fact explanation must be that these are dancers adjusting their costumes in the wings before going on, we cannot locate them in relation to the stage or even the items of (presumably) theatrical scenery. The effect is slightly unreal but intensely poetic. Degas' failing eyesight may have been solely responsible for the change, but it is also possible that resemblances between works of this sort and paintings by Degas's contemporaries, Cézanne, Gauguin and van Gogh, are not entirely coincidental.

At the Milliner's c.1905-10

Pastel on paper

▷ *Overleaf page 78*

DEGAS ENJOYED going shopping with women friends such as the American painter Mary Cassatt. In the early 1880s he produced a series of works, mostly pastels, set in millinery shops. As always, what interested him most was how people moved, though he also exploited the decorative possibilities of the hats, rising up like blossoms on their stands. These elements became even more important when he returned briefly to the subject in his purblind old age, working from earlier studies and his wonderful visual memory. Here, detail is almost completely eliminated, and the picture might almost be an abstract, comprising areas of intense colour and texture. Nevertheless the central figure of the milliner is charged with an energy which is reinforced by the stand in front of her arm, creating a dizzying spiral effect. Clearly, while he could paint and draw at all, Degas could still create masterpieces.

ACKNOWLEDGEMENTS

The Publisher would like to thank the following for their kind permission to reproduce the paintings in this book:

Bridgeman Art Library, London 58; /**Barber Institute, Birmingham** 57; /**Birmingham City Museums and Art Gallery** 9; /**Burrell Collection, Glasgow** 66-67; /**Courtauld Institute Galleries, University of London** 38; /**Giraudon /Municipal Museum of Art, Kitakyushu** 26-27; /**Giraudon /Musée d'Orsay, Paris** 16, 29, 30-31, 39, 50-51, 54, 63, 68-69, 78; /**Giraudon /Museu Calouste Gulbenkian** 14; /**Glasgow Art Gallery and Museum** 34-35, 59, 64; /**Hermitage, St. Petersburg** 75; /**Lauros-Giraudon /Musée d'Orsay, Paris** 20-21; /**Lefevre Gallery, London** 62; /**Louvre, Paris** 10-11; /**Henry P. McIlhenny, Philadelphia** 24-25; /**Metropolitan Museum of Art, New York** 19, 36-37; /**Minneapolis Society of Fine Arts, Minnesota, USA** 28; /**Musée des Beaux Arts, Lyons** 49; /**Musée des Beaux Arts, Pau** 32-33; /**Musée Bonnat, Bayonne** 15; /**Musée d'Orsay, Paris** 23, 41, 42, 48, 52-53, 61; /**Museu Calouste Gulbenkian, Lisbon** 56; /**National Gallery, London** 12-13, 17, 44, 55, 71, 72-73; /**National Gallery of Scotland, Edinburgh** 60, 74; /**Pushkin Museum, Moscow** 40, 76; /**Tate Gallery, London** 47, 70; /**By Courtesy of the Board of Trustees of the V & A** 46.